Our Carbon Footprint

COLOURED VERSION

CHILDREN SAVING OUR PLANET SERIES

CAROL SUTTERS

AuthorHouse™ UK
1663 Liberty Drive
Bloomington, IN 47403 USA
www.authorhouse.co.uk
UK TFN: 0800 0148641 (Toll Free inside the UK)
UK Local: 02036 956322 (+44 20 3695 6322 from outside the UK)

Because of the dynamic nature of the Internet, any web addresses or links contained in this book may have changed since publication and may no longer be valid. The views expressed in this work are solely those of the author and do not necessarily reflect the views of the publisher, and the publisher hereby disclaims any responsibility for them.

Any people depicted in stock imagery provided by Getty Images are models, and such images are being used for illustrative purposes only. Certain stock imagery © Getty Images.

This book is printed on acid-free paper.

ISBN: 978-1-6655-8797-6 (sc)
ISBN: 978-1-6655-8798-3 (e)

Library of Congress Control Number: 2021906672

Print information available on the last page.

Published by AuthorHouse 04/21/2021

authorHOUSE®

The children returned home from holiday and mum recalled it was important that they should understand about travel and our carbon footprint. This had been mentioned by mum when they travelled to the seaside by a new type of train. This particular train was powered by electricity, which had been generated by wind turbines and not by coal. Steam trains originally were powered by coal which is fossil fuel. Carbon emissions from transport account for almost thirty per cent of global warming. Mum wants to also tell them about global attempts to cut carbon emissions.

After their discussions, mum suggests the children should think of some examples of how we could reduce our carbon footprint in travel and other activities. She begins, *"You will remember that burning carbon in fossil fuels uses up a valuable resource from the earth, which takes millions of years to replace. Also, carbon dioxide gas causes the temperature to rise in the air and seas and it makes the oceans more acidic. All these effects damage natural ecosystems for plants and animals across the world.*

Waste plant   Greenhouse

Greenhouse gases occur naturally but human activity increases the normal levels. Carbon dioxide is a greenhouse gas and it is released into the air when coal, oil and natural gas are burned, such as in coal power stations. Carbon is responsible for the largest carbon footprint. Methane and nitrous oxide are other greenhouse gases. Large amounts of carbon and other greenhouse gases come from industrial processes and waste management such as landfill dumps. Also human activity such as driving cars, heating our houses and flying in aeroplanes emits extra greenhouse gases. These cause climate warming."

Mum continues, "*Sometimes people calculate a journey to be carbon neutral by trying to replace the carbon dioxide pollution their journey causes. This is a plan to offset a carbon footprint. For example, they calculate the carbon dioxide produced by a flight and then counteract this by planting enough trees. The trees will in time produce more oxygen into the atmosphere, to balance the carbon dioxide produced. This is called achieving a carbon neutral balance.*"

"Sea grass meadows, mangroves and coastal wetlands have been found to be better than trees at trapping carbon. Seagrass leaves form large, dense meadows under the sea. They provide the basis of many ocean fisheries. Like coral reefs and tropical rainforests, these underwater gardens are full of life. Seagrass meadows provide food and habitat for thousands of species such as shellfish, seahorses, parrotfish and sea turtles. Seagrass captures carbon through the water via its bright green leaves and stores it in its roots. It is 35 times better than tropical forests at trapping carbon. A million seagrass seeds have been planted off the coast of Pembrokeshire. This meadow will boost fish numbers, support marine life and reduce carbon dioxide."

"The Antarctic ice shelf ecosystem plays a very important role in balancing the climate of the world. Life in the Antarctic seas may soak up much more carbon than the Amazon rain forest. The oceans take up carbon dioxide as it dissolves in water, but also phytoplankton in water take up carbon dioxide for photosynthesis. These are tiny plants and algae."

"However," Mum advised, "In some countries trees are being actively destroyed. This includes palm trees to provide palm oil for vegetable oil in food, biscuits and cosmetics. This causes deforestation of some of the world's precious biodiverse forests and endangers species such as the orangutan, and pygmy elephant."

"In 2015 the landmark United Nations Paris Agreement was launched to limit climate change. This is a legal global treaty to limit global warming to below 2 degrees and preferably to 1.5 degrees Celsius, compared to pre-industrial levels. Countries in the Paris Agreement are required to make many social and technological changes costing money. They will make plans to tackle climate change problems based on science. Every 5 years each plan will state how targets to reduce greenhouse gas emissions are being met, as well as actions to cope with rising temperatures. China, USA, India and Russia are the highest carbon emitters and need to take urgent action. They will also need to assist poorer nations with science and technology skills to combat rising temperature. Many countries have committed to net zero carbon emissions, including the UK, by 2050. The next United Nations Climate talks will be COP26 in Glasgow in November 2021. This will bring together heads of state, climate scientists and campaigners to agree action we can all take to tackle the climate change emergency. These plans will help stop the adverse effects of climate change on our world."

"The UK Parliament has set up Citizens' Assemblies which are gatherings of people to discuss and help the leaders in parliament to reach carbon targets. The UK has pledged to reduce carbon emissions by 78% based on 1990, by the year 2035. This will be a major part of the Children's Revolt towards saving the Planet called Extinction Rebellion."

"In the UK, part of the plan to achieve the carbon emission reduction target means that new diesel and petrol cars will be phased out by 2035. Electric cars will replace them. Other industries are trying to reduce or balance carbon emissions."

Mum also reported, "The National Trust, which helps to preserve many woodlands and rivers, has a target to plant 20 million trees by 2030, as well as maintaining peat bogs, to help counteract carbon emissions."

"In Switzerland one Company is capturing the carbon dioxide from burning waste rubbish plants and piping it to nearby greenhouses to increase vegetable crop production. This means no carbon dioxide is lost to the atmosphere so the system is carbon neutral."

"Sustainable aviation fuel is a clean substitute for fossil jet fuels. It is not developed from petrol, but by liquid fuels from agricultural and household waste and used cooking oil. They use sources that can be maintained and which do not disturb the ecological balance. Airlines combine these sustainable aviation fuels with kerosene, for example, to reduce use of fossil fuels and reduce their carbon footprint. It is part of the plan for aeroplanes to reduce their carbon emissions."

"In trying to reduce our carbon footprint we try to find ways of doing things which consume less energy."

Tom says, "We could cycle more and travel less by car. There are even electric bikes."

Kate adds, "We could switch to using solar panels for electricity and not that generated from coal powered electricity stations."

Can you think of more examples to reduce your carbon footprint? The children wrote down the following suggestions:

- Eat less red meat and dairy products.

- Eat food grown locally and in season, which does not have to be transported from long distances abroad.

- Buy less food wrapped in plastic packaging that is difficult to recycle.

- Dry clothes on a line, so that we avoid using an electric clothes dryer.

- Plant a garden or trees.

- Grow your own vegetables.

- Do not keep buying fashion clothes and quickly throwing them away. You can also recycle clothes.

- Create less waste.

- Walk to school, rather than drive.

Mum congratulates them, "*Very good examples Kate and Tom. Major companies have made pledges to reduce their carbon footprint to reduce pollution. Examples include paper coffee cups without plastic straws, converting to more non-fossil fuel energy sources, using less plastic packaging and sourcing materials locally rather than from abroad. Also, by having more meetings via teleconferencing rather than all gathering at a conference in a foreign country.*"

What did we learn today? (tick the box if you understood and agree)

☐ Carbon dioxide is a very important damaging greenhouse gas. Increased levels are responsible for climate change and for damaging ecosystems.

☐ We should be aware of our carbon footprint in our daily activities to try to reduce it to save our planet.

☐ Simple actions such as reducing food waste, walking, biking, not over eating and using cars and planes less, can reduce a person's carbon footprint.

☐ Governments are trying to make whole countries achieve a net zero carbon balance by 2050 to preserve the plants and animals on earth and reset biodiversity.

Kate and Tom learn about fires destroying the planet in the Amazon, Australia and Paradise in Canada in book 12 Fire Fire.

Children Saving our Planet Series

Books

1. **Tom and Kate Go to Westminster**

2. **Kate and Tom Learn About Fossil Fuels**

3. **Tom and Kate Chose Green Carbon**

4. **Tress and Deforestation**

5. **Our Neighbourhood Houses**

6. **Our Neighbourhood Roads**

7. **Shopping at the Farm Shop**

8. **Travelling to a Holiday by the Sea**

9. **Picnic at the Seaside on Holiday**

10. **The Oceans and Coral**

11. **Our Carbon Footprint**

12. **Fire Fire**

13. **The Antarctic Warms Up**

14. **The Canada Catastrophe**

15. **The Coronavirus and saving the Planet**

16. **The Children's Rebellion and Climate Change**

These series of simple books explain the landmark importance of Children's participation in the Extinction rebellion protest. Children actively want to encourage and support adults to urgently tackle both the Climate and the Biodiversity emergencies. The booklets enable children at an early age to understand some of the scientific principles that are affecting the destruction of the planet. If global political and economic systems fail to address the climate emergency, the responsibility will rest upon children to save the Planet for themselves.

This series is dedicated to

Theodore, Aria and Ophelia.

Printed in the United States
by Baker & Taylor Publisher Services